GREAT
SPORTING
MOMENTS

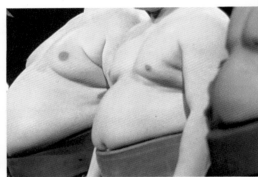

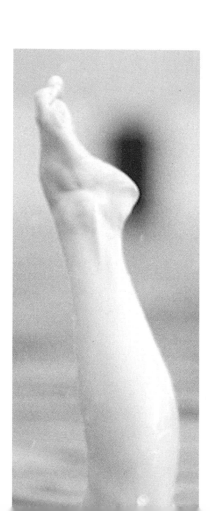

GREAT
SPORTING MOMENTS

DAVID THOMAS

with Mike Barfield and John Langdon
on the substitutes' bench

Fontana/Collins

First published in 1989 by Fontana Paperbacks
8 Grafton Street, London W1X 3LA

Copyright © D. T. Productions Ltd 1989
Photograph of St Paul's Cathedral © Barnaby's Picture Library;
all other photographs © Allsport.

Printed and bound in Great Britain by
William Collins Sons & Co. Ltd., Glasgow

I bet she drinks Carling Black Label.

'I'll get the bastard that nicked my Lucozade.'

The Auchtermuchty and District Men's Formation Rumba Squad – arguably the least successful and worst-dressed team in the history of ballroom dancing.

Bobby Robson is stunned. He can't remember the last time the England team put four balls in the net.

Nigel Mansell is fed up with his Ferrari breaking down. So he's trying something a little more reliable for his next Grand Prix.

The New Zealand All Blacks are past masters at intimidation. Before an international they refuse to wash for a month, then flash their armpits at the opposition.

Here's Mike Tyson showing off his trophies: 'And *this* one I got off a Volkswagen Golf.'

Following his Olympic triumph a Bulgarian weightlifter receives his reward – the first instalment on his Skoda.

Skating champ Katarina Witt has a lovely personality. She always lets defeated opponents kiss her on both cheeks.

In a desperate bid to beat striking Spanish air-traffic controllers, plucky British holiday-makers parachute into Benidorm.

QUESTION TIME   1

Is this the Greyhound Derby? Or just the auditions to replace Joan Rivers?

QUESTION TIME   2

Is this a top skier blasting through powder snow? Or simply Frank Bough sneezing?

QUESTION TIME   3

Which of you bitches is my mother?

Nick Faldo didn't do too well at this year's British Open, so he's pinning his hopes on a new sport – juggling badminton rackets.

After a tragic attempt to escape Christopher Dean, Jayne Torvill is shot by East German guards when almost over the border.

Wrestler Les Kellet asks himself the big question: 'How much longer do I have to keep doing this before they give me my Equity card?'

The MIKE TYSON'S Girlfriend Elimination Stakes

Fig. 1

With the departure of former wife, Robin Givens, Mike Tyson has been searching for a possible replacement. Vast numbers of women have applied for the role of mate to a man worth up to $100 million, and so a complex selection procedure has been evolved to filter out unsuitable candidates.

The following sequence reveals the process with scientific precision.

First, would-be Tyson Totties are dropped 5,000 feet from the Goodyear blimp (Fig. 1) so as to test their resistance to heavy blows.

Survivors then mud-wrestle (Fig. 2) for the right to go through to the final training round . . . which involves accurate simulation of Tyson's lovemaking technique (Fig. 3).

Only one candidate will survive long enough to be winched down onto Tyson's double bed . . . while the champ himself waits expectantly in the corner (Fig. 5).

Fig. 2

Fig. 3

Fig. 4

Fig. 5

MEDALLION MAD

Most Olympic events require years of dedication, intensive training and large numbers of drugs. They have no relevance to the lives of the slobs and swots who watch them on the telly and who are apt to feel, well, a bit left out. With this in mind, the International Olympic Committee is planning to bring in a new range of events designed to appeal to ordinary men and women. For example...

The Women's Spearing—the—Cocktail—Sausage

The Men's Pizza Chuck

The Men's Indoor Barbecue (including medals for the Burger Burn, the Chicken Thigh Freestyle and the Individual Menu)

The Men's Outdoor Nose-Blow

The Men's Marathon Cocktail Mix

The Men's Outdoor Nose-Blow
With Compulsory Aeroplane
Impression

The Women's Synchronized
Shakespeare (including
amongst its compulsory figures
the speech, 'Is this a beach ball I
see before me?')

To the Manners Born
A Guide to Sporting Etiquette

Many people have complained about the decline in sportsmanship and good manners in modern sport. But as these four pictures demonstrate, there are still some people who believe in the benefits of proper behaviour and personal hygiene.

As Ian Botham shows, it's never too late to gargle with mouthwash.

Top jockeys use an automatic polisher to keep their horses' shoes sparkling clean.

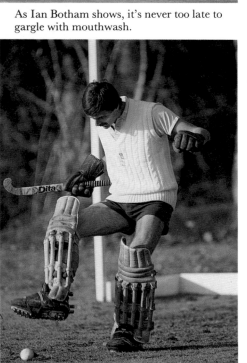

Gary Lineker explains the benefits of dental floss to his eager new Tottenham teammates. ▶

Hockey goalkeeper Ian Taylor is always careful to extinguish his cigarette before attempting to stop the ball. ◀

THE GREAT SPORTING MOMENTS

MURRAY WALKER

MEMORIAL PILEUP

RACING CARS

DESIGNED BY COMPUTERS

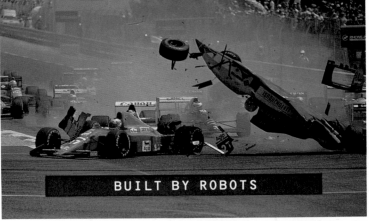

BUILT BY ROBOTS

DRIVEN BY RADIO ONE DEEJAYS

Russian gymnast Marina Lobach confounds the
sceptics: 'Yes! We have toilet paper . . . and we know
how to use it.'

Mike Tyson may have knocked out Frank Bruno. But
there's no way he'll beat Frank's mother.

A Japanese tourist discovers just how tough it can be shopping in Harrods' sports department at the height of the winter sale.

In an attempt to make televised bowls more exciting, this year's world championship will feature a new event – freestyle floor exercises.

This is not a terrible fall at a three-day event. This is in fact the first horse in the world to own a human yo-yo.

In yet another blow for beleaguered London Transport, jockeys are complaining that they can't get their horses through the new barriers on the tube.

Lucky, the world's fastest greyhound, hides from the Seoul Olympic caterers.

Motorcycling's a tough sport. Here French star Christian Sarron fails in a bid to rugby-tackle the opposition.

Baseball administrators report a new form of crowd trouble — Barry White keeps invading the pitch.

British sports fans have traditionally concentrated on favourite national pastimes like rugby, cricket and fat men in nylon shirts throwing little pointed sticks at the wall. But thanks to the expansion of televised sport, we are now more aware than ever of the pleasures of games we'd never even heard of until Channel 4 realized they couldn't afford to show First Division football.

Great Sporting Moments has travelled the world to bring you the low-down on three such sports, starting with . . .

THE GAMES PEOPLE PLAY

AMERICAN FOOTBALL

There are still a few people who think that the Super Bowl is a really nice bit of kitchen china. They reckon a Strong Safety is a particularly absorbent baby's nappy. And they're sure that a Tight End is what you get from a Jane Fonda work-out.

We want to help these people. Which is why we went to Chicago to compile this photo-report on the Bear necessities (sorry about that) of American footballing knowledge, as follows . . .

1. Pre-Match Preparation
Before any big game, the players have to memorize an incredibly complicated gameplan. Then, and only then, are they allowed to look at this week's Cheerleader Centrefold.

2. Uniform Maintenance
(a) The man on the bench is not, as you might imagine, the player with the most offensive bad breath. He is, in fact, the Rear End Coordinator. He has the vital task of checking the other team-members for signs of Visible Panty Line.

(b) Note how tragically visible panties can threaten a player's career.

VPL – A REAL PARROT-SICKENER FOR ANY TOP PRO.

3. The Huddle

It is a little-known fact that almost all star American footballers are actually Freemasons. Here they exchange their secret handshake.

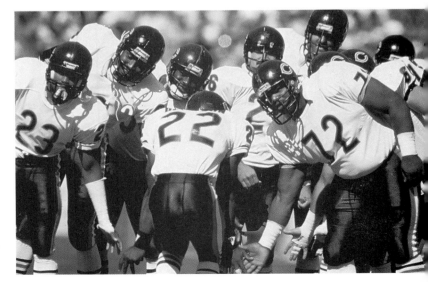

4. Team Spirit

Genital stroking is an excellent way of raising a player's morale. And other things besides.

5. Nutrition

Big players can weigh as much as 5 tons. In order to maintain their stature they have an extraordinary diet, which may include such items as Elephant Cutlets, Whale Blubber Fricassee and Creamed Walrus Fat. Here William Perry demonstrates how he came by his famous nickname: nothing stands between him and a full refrigerator.

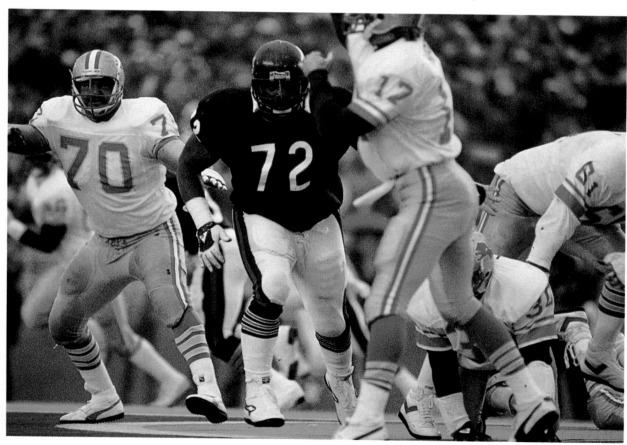

6. Public Relations
Interviews with the media are a key part of any sportsman's life. But Walter Payton's having a hard time telling his coach why he's having a press conference before the game's even ended.

7. Cheerleaders
Lovely cheerleaders are one of the game's biggest audience attractions. The Bear girls, however, are unique: their pom-poms are made from The Refrigerator's nasal hair.

Of course, although American footballers are pretty big, they look like pussycats next to ...

SUMO
SUMAS
SUMAT

The Sumo code of honour is an integral part of traditional Japanese life, and its customs reflect the culture of the Orient. In Fig. 1, for example, a Sumo wrestler throws monosodium glutamate onto his dinner.

What do they eat? Well, Fig. 2 shows two Sumo stars with a typical day's food.

Fig. 1

Fig. 2

Fig. 3

Fig. 5

As well as eating together, they share their sleeping and sexual arrangements. In Fig. 3 we see a group of wrestlers preparing their leg-over technique. While Fig. 4 shows two top men fighting on their double bed to see who gets to lie on the damp spot.

Japan, of course, is forbidden nuclear weapons. But, as Fig. 5 demonstrates, they do have other means of getting their way at international summits. They simply wheel in a Sumo wrestler and threaten that he'll flash at the Heads of State unless their demands are met in full.

Fig. 4

Nothing could be further removed from Sumo than the grace, the elegance and the shiny swimsuits of . . .

There can't be many sports whose contestants have to put on girly costumes, slap on a ton of make-up and maintain a permanent daft grin. Men's ice-skating, however, does not feature in this book, so we'll just have to make do with something almost as stupid – synchronized swimming.

Many people feel that this so-called sport is a conspiracy by male chauvinist pigs who want to make women look as ridiculous as possible. Nevertheless, it is immensely popular (perhaps because there are millions of chauvy pigs who like to see women looking ridiculous), so in this section we attempt to answer some of your questions about it all . . .

1. **How do girls become synchronized swimmers?**

There are a number of different ways into the sport. These two were runners-up in Paul Daniels' recent search for a new assistant. Then they realized that their talents for standing around in foolish poses could be put to medal-winning use.

2. **Why do they wear those plugs in their noses?**

A number of reasons. British champ Amanda Dodd, for example, wears hers because government cutbacks have forced her to train at a local sewage works.

3. **Is Amanda the only British swimmer to suffer this way?**

Afraid not; the United Kingdom formation synchro team have to practise in a car park.

Synchronized Silliness

4. Is this a more fortunate formation synchro team?
No, this is a group of sky-divers who happen to have landed in a swimming pool.

5. So what can British synchro-swimmers do to raise money?
Sponsorship seems to be the answer. This shot shows our game girls trying to raise funds from the British Chiropodists' Association.

Is that all?
No, we've got one more picture for you.

6. What, that one of two girls practising their routine?
No, that one of two girls practising how to head-butt their opponents.

It's a terrible sight — an out-and-out basket case.

It's Mike Tyson again, doing his favourite impressions: 'And *this* is my Larry Adler.'

Sexual Positions in Sport: No. 1, The Sjoberg Shag. Top Swedish high jumper Patrick Sjoberg has abandoned the limp old Fosbury flop. Now he just lies on his back and thinks of Sweden.

Swedish gymnast Helena Rosander is unique: she's the only girl in the world to train on the London Underground.

Eric Bristow's delighted. He's finally found a cup that'll hold ten pints at a time.

Are Californian cheerleaders
natural blondes?

Fatima Whitbread likes to take a
foreign holiday between big
competitions. This is her moving
Crete back into position.

the FRANK BRUNO training manual

It takes an awful lot to become a boxer of Frank Bruno's class — and we don't just mean years and years of easy fights against clapped-out opponents. If you want that one big chance, that 'I coulda been a contender' moment, you've got to be prepared to go through the same gruelling preparation as Big Frank.

His full training manual includes the following vital skills:

1. Learning to duck.

2. Learning to ignore criticism.

3. Learning to count to ten.

It's that Mansell again; Nigel's just realized that motor-racing is exactly like robbing banks. You stick a stocking over your head, leap into the fastest car you can find and drive away with millions.

 # BERKS ON BIKES

This year's Channel 4 coverage of the *Tour de France* was exhaustingly exhaustive. It showed you everything you could possibly want to see. Everything, that is, except for the following scenes, which no one in their right mind would want to see, but which we're going to show you anyway . . .

The race started well with the strongly-fancied Vatican team hoping to gain divine support by riding in the shape of the cross.

The British team did as badly as had been expected. At one point they were overtaken by a group of trees . . .

Le Tour de France

. . . and even borrowing Concorde could do little to improve their time.

The surrealist team came disguised as a thousand-gallon bottle of wine . . .

. . . while the Irish came a cropper after attempting a mid-race game of Twister.

There were a number of dangers facing the riders. Coke dealers were everywhere . . .

. . . and bicycle thieves stole racers' wheels at the slightest opportunity.

Influenced, perhaps, by all the drugs on offer, one man became convinced he was a Big Mac. So he poured tomato sauce all over his face and wore his hair in a bun.

CRICKET, *LOUSY* CRICKET

Typical of England's South Africans is Allan Lamb. He is a ruthless, dedicated professional. Here, for example, we see him going flat out to prepare for his next Test appearance.

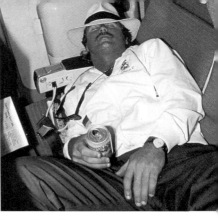

Look, we're sorry, all right. We've been trying to avoid this and we almost made it. But, no matter how painful this subject might be, there's no getting away from the fact that you can't have a book called *Great Sporting Moments* and publish it in England and leave out cricket.

What? Well, fair enough. You've got us bang to rights. We are, it's true, in breach of the Trade Descriptions Act by including the English cricket team. They aren't great. They aren't sporting. And the only moments they have are disastrous ones.

But the publishers think that there are still a few people out there who'd like to look at silly pictures of England cricketers. And they're paying the money, so what they want they get.

Now, the first thing to consider about English cricket is South Africa. English cricketers are not allowed to play in South Africa. If they play in South Africa they are banned from test matches (which must, quite frankly, come as a relief), and if they then get picked for England there are riots and demos and the team is prevented from playing the West Indies in half the islands of the Caribbean.

But although English cricketers are not allowed to play in South Africa, South African players are allowed to play in England. And, what's more, they're allowed to play *for* England, too. In fact, they're positively encouraged to play for England because they're so much better than the English.

But even a top pro has to let off steam. So here's Allan fooling around in fancy dress . . .

. . . before getting back into his usual gear.

What an inspiration Lamby is. Almost as much as David Gower, the man who keeps being made Captain of England, even though he's as blind as a batsman and keeps making a spectacle of himself.

And then there's Ian Botham, the man whose Farrah Fawcett haircut put the highlights back into cricket.
Bet he uses Harmony hairspray. But pity the fielder: he has to duck the dandruff.

John McEnroe has long been one of the best-known sportspeople in the world. But who can say what goes on inside that tortured mind of his? No one can, but we're going to anyway.

John has often been accused of gamesmanship. For example, he often puts off his opponent by means of his unique joke-shop tennis racket. ◁

He has also had a stormy relationship ▷ with umpires. Here he demonstrates the appropriately grovelling posture he expects them to adopt in his presence.

ATTACK

A little later, he runs through his own △ unique brand of excuses: 'A worm put me off . . . I can hear trains in the distance . . . there's got to be a coal mine under here somewhere.'

In recent years Mac has been attempting a comeback. This dramatic picture demonstrates one reason why it has been less successful than he might have hoped – his hand-eye coordination has completely gone to pot. ▷

This might drive some men to despair. In fact this picture, showing him bending over with his head in his hands and an agonized expression on his face, appears to illustrate that. It is, however, just his Bobby Robson impersonation.

So does *this* shot show the depths of McEnroe's unhappiness? No, it shows him applying for sponsorship from Armitage Shanks.

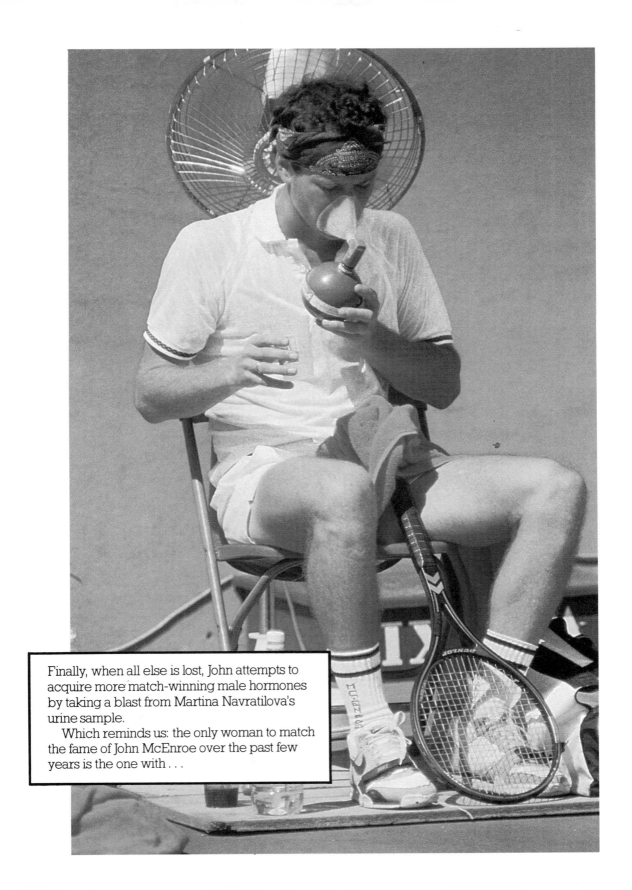

Finally, when all else is lost, John attempts to acquire more match-winning male hormones by taking a blast from Martina Navratilova's urine sample.

Which reminds us: the only woman to match the fame of John McEnroe over the past few years is the one with . . .

MARTINA'S MUSCLES

What an amazing decade it's been for Martina Navratilova. As she comes towards the twilight of her career, the eight-times Wimbledon champion can look back over such memorable moments as . . .

The time she went on *The Antiques Road Show.*

Her brilliant performance on *One Man and Her Dog.*

Her attempted defection from Czechoslovakia to the Japanese Davis Cup squad, and . . .

Her attempt to beat John McEnroe to the Armitage Shanks sponsorship.

And for one final look at the world of tennis, just turn the page to find your very own official *Great Sporting Moments* A–Z Guide of British Tennis Winners . . .

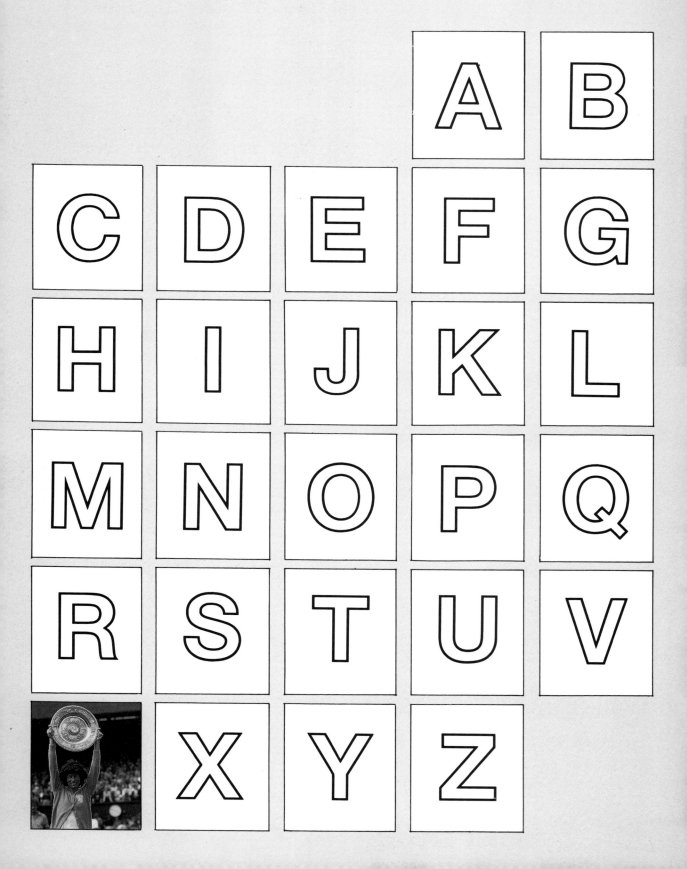

The man in the middle manages ►
the West German football team.
But which of the other two stands
the best chance of getting
England to a World Cup Final?

There are lots of round shiny ▲
things in this photo. But how
many of them are snooker balls?

KIDDIE KOMPETITION KORNER

Now children, just look at these pictures and see if
you can answer the simple questions . . .

Here is a man with a horsey.
Which do you think has the
higher IQ?

Can you spot
Robert Maxwell?

Contrary to popular rumour, Colonel Gaddafi has not joined the Australian hockey team.

Well, here's one way of combating sexual harassment.

Urine some, u-lose some. Richard Fox is delighted: he's just broken the world record for the largest-ever urine sample.

Nick Faldo's caddy dispenses some wise advice:
'If it's a trout, I'd hit it with a four-iron.'

Meanwhile, Sevvy Ballesteros re-enacts
a recent meeting with Roy Hattersley.

*The latest sports craze to sweep America is
Burgerball. Contestants have to eat a
hamburger with their hands tied behind their
backs. This man had no trouble with the burger.
It was the ketchup he couldn't manage.*

In a historic triumph, British mountaineers have succeeded in climbing . . .

the North Face of Mike Tyson's neck . . .

the Lower Face of Mike Tyson's jaw . . .

and the Lifted Face of Britt Ekland.

The Nottingham Forest manager is known all over the world: 'This is my impression of Brian Clough's mouth.'

'Oi! Ref! Look at that blatant tackle!'

Women's rugby differs from the male version in a number of respects. The main picture, for example, does not show a scrum. This is, in fact, the latest thing in natural childbirth.

Meanwhile, the inset shot demonstrates one of the hazards of the game – a terrible injury to a player's mascara.

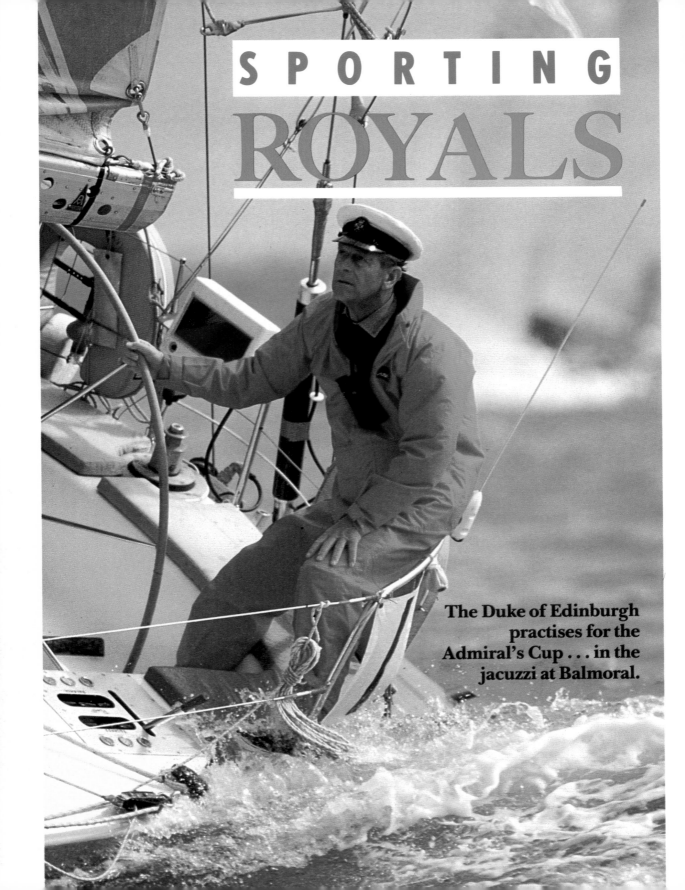

SPORTING
ROYALS

The Duke of Edinburgh
practises for the
Admiral's Cup . . . in the
jacuzzi at Balmoral.

We have a wonderful Royal Family. OK, so none of them is likely to win *Mastermind* in a hurry. But when it comes to riding or shooting dumb animals, they're the tops. And their passionate devotion to sport doesn't stop with huntin' and shootin' and fishin', as these pictures show . . .

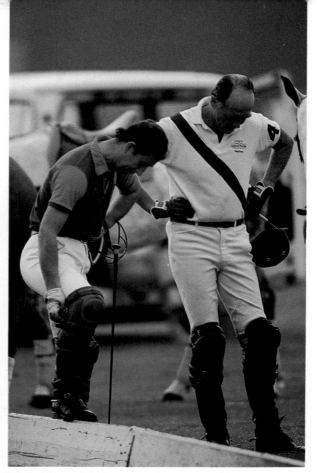

Major Ronald Ferguson has a consoling message for an injured Prince Charles: 'If it's still hurting, Sir, I think I know where you could go to get it massaged.'

A key moment in any Royal holiday – the Queen picks her five-a-side football team.

And now back to the Duke of Edinburgh – a man whose language is so strong his horses have to wear earmuffs.

Meanwhile, tickets are scarce for the Royal Box at Wimbledon. So scarce, in fact, that Fergie has to smuggle in Princess Michael under her dress.

Prince Edward is the 'artistic' member of the family, but even he can be a sporting winner. Here he receives the Lloyd Webber Samovar for services to Olympic Teamaking.

This is a nostalgic memory from the Royal Photo Album – the time they forgot the key to the portaloo at Badminton.

Poor Anne, nothing could stop her coming a cropper here. Experts are divided as to what this picture illustrates. It could be:
  (a) a bad fall at Badminton
  (b) a demonstration of how *not* to take a horse through an automatic car-wash
  (c) a failed attempt to ride down the water-splash at Alton Towers

SPORTING HEAD CASES

In the history of man's sporting endeavours, three barmy barnets have boldly grown where no hair has grown before. Or not, depending. They are . . .

THE KEVIN KEEGAN KISS-KURL
A quick glance at this shot shows that, no matter who influenced Keegan's footballing style, the biggest influence on his hairstyle was . . . Bonnie Langford.

But for Keegan, there was more to personal grooming than mere hair care. Below he tends to a team-mate with his trusty bucket of Brut 33.

THE BOBBY CHARLTON BASKET WEAVE

There was a time when Bobby Charlton almost had a full head of hair. And this picture, dating from the mid-fourteenth century, proves it.

In later years, however, he developed his world-famous 'single strand' approach. His one remaining hair was knitted into a skullcap by a team of blind Bulgarian basket weavers, who guaranteed complete scalp coverage in anything up to a force 5 wind. (Note how Bobby's parting is still above his ear in this picture. Later it would descend, coming to a halt just below his left nipple.)

THE DUNCAN GOODHEW DOME

Duncan Goodhew has the only sporting head to carry Prince Charles's official seal of approval. Clever Duncan based his uniquely rug-resistant scalp on Sir Christopher Wren's historic design for the dome of St Paul's Cathedral.

Terrible haircuts are one of the great terrors of sport, but even they are as nothing compared with the great menace facing sport today. That menace is . . .

DRUG-CRAZED SPORTSWOMEN FROM HELL

Or even from East Germany. Recent reports have claimed that East German women were force-fed steroids that made them world champions . . . but at a terrible price.

One side effect was that they became desperate for sex. So it wasn't all bad. But the treatments led to a living hell of irreversible side effects. Our exclusive picture report tells the story of one such East German girl, little Anna Bolik.

It's 1973, and Anna is a happy, normal 10-year-old gymnast, competing in her national junior championships.

National coaches spot Anna's track potential and she switches to athletics. But in 1981 she still seems a typical, healthy teenager.

Little does Anna know, however, that her strawberries and cream have been spiked with drugs.

The first clue that
something is
wrong emerges
at the '83 World
Championships.
Anna looks lean
and strong. And
women begin to
chase after her.

Two years later
and Anna, now
Andy, runs for
East Germany in
the Men's 400m.

By the time of the 1985 European
Indoor Championships, Anna has
developed powerful biceps, a flat chest
. . . and an extraordinary quantity of
underarm hair.

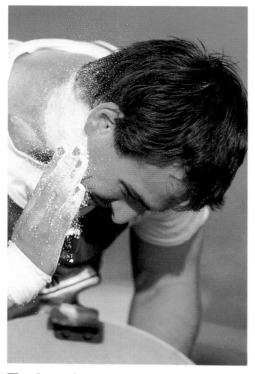

The drugs keep coming, often in powdered form, and Anna/Andy's body keeps expanding.

He goes to Seoul as a shot-putter.

1989; Andy Bolik lives in Dresden with his wife Heidi and his daughter Anna. East German coaches have already visited the little girl. They feed her strawberries and cream.

Anna Jr. enters her first international event and the ghastly cycle begins all over again.

But is East Germany the only country to give its athletes drugs? Obviously not. Ben Johnson has been found guilty of drug-taking. And questions have also been asked about the amazing Florence Griffith Joyner.

Feminine Flo-Jo strongly denies all the allegations . . .

. . . but, looking at this picture, can we be sure?

And what about England's sporting stars? Can it be any coincidence that all our most successful sportsmen are incredibly boring people? Is there some substance, as yet unknown to the authorities, which can guarantee a winning performance, but only at the cost of draining all life from a player's personality?

Look at the following pictures, consider the evidence, and then ask yourself: What are they on?

Nigel Mansell: a demon in a car, a dullard out of it. Is this man one tyre short of a set, or what?

Steve Davis: note the blank expression, the dull stare, the dodgy dicky-bow tie.

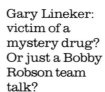

Gary Lineker: victim of a mystery drug? Or just a Bobby Robson team talk?

And finally . . .

THE REAR END OF THE BOOK

And now, over to Bill Beaumont's team . . . any idea who this might be? Here's a clue: the owner always liked to give it their best shot. No ideas? Well, it's obvious, isn't it. . .

Yes, of course, it's Geoff Capes, Olympic shot-
putter and Britain's most celebrated skirt-wearing
strongman.

Needle Crafts 18

CROSS-STITCH

SEARCH PRESS
Tunbridge Wells

Cross-stitch embroidery is a simple counted-thread technique usually worked on an evenweave or linen-type fabric, with the stitches forming a pattern on the fabric. History shows that cross-stitch has been one of the most widely used stitches in the decoration of national costume and household linen, but it is a stitch which has been largely neglected by modern embroiderers.

This book describes and illustrates the basic techniques and methods of cross-stitch embroidery on fabric (not on canvas), and the development of new and free uses of cross-stitch in contemporary designs to achieve many different effects.

THE STITCH

A cross stitch is just two straight stitches in the form of a diagonal cross. Traditionally it was always a square stitch, taken over the same number of threads in each direction, and worked in several different ways depending upon the design. The only unbreakable rule in cross-stitch is that all the top stitches should lie in the same direction.

Single crosses

Each cross is worked individually, the first stitch going diagonally from bottom right to top left, and the second stitch diagonally from bottom left to top right (Fig. 1).

Horizontal rows

A continuous row of crosses may be made in two stages – work the first diagonal stitches from right to left along the row, and return working the stitches from left to right to complete the crosses. This method is generally used for borders or backgrounds, whereas individual motifs are worked in single crosses. The disadvantage of working in rows is that it is more difficult to unpick an area if this should become necessary (Fig. 2).

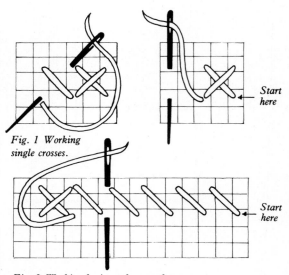

Start here

Fig. 1 Working single crosses.

Start here

Fig. 2 Working horizontal rows of crosses. Start here

Vertical rows

Each cross is worked individually. All the stitches on the reverse side of the work are vertical (Fig. 3).

Diagonal rows

When working in ascending or descending diagonal lines, it is easier to count the threads vertically and then horizontally, than to try and count them diagonally (Fig. 4: a, b).

Starting and finishing the thread

Whichever the method of working, begin by knotting the thread and passing the needle to the back of the fabric approximately 1in. (2.5cm) from the intended starting point – the knot will rest on the surface and the first few stitches will cover the end on the back (Fig. 5). Later on the knot can be cut off. Fasten off by darning the thread through the stitches on the back.

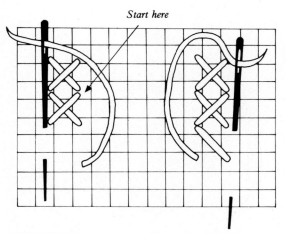

Fig. 3 Working vertical rows of crosses.

a) Left to right   Start here

b) Right to left   Start here

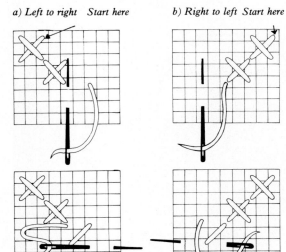

Fig. 4 Working diagonal rows of crosses.

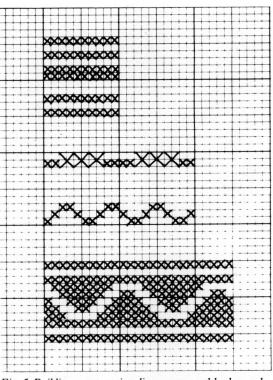

Fig. 5 Building crosses up into lines, curves and backgrounds.

Page 4:
Neapolitan ice motif – *a small design worked in coton à broder on fine evenweave linen (Dorothy Wooding).*

Strawberry sweet – *a motif and a border based on a candy, worked on evenweave linen using a fine perle thread and Danish Flower threads. The cross-stitches are worked over different numbers of threads (Mary Tasker).*

Page 5:
Dress *with applied cross-stitch bands, worked with a traditional German cross stitch motif (Heidi Jenkins).*

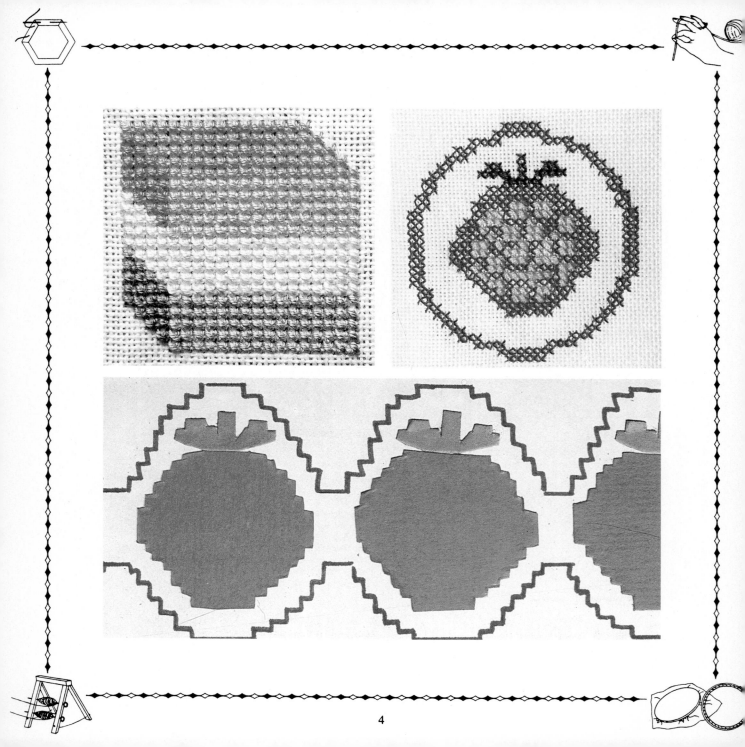

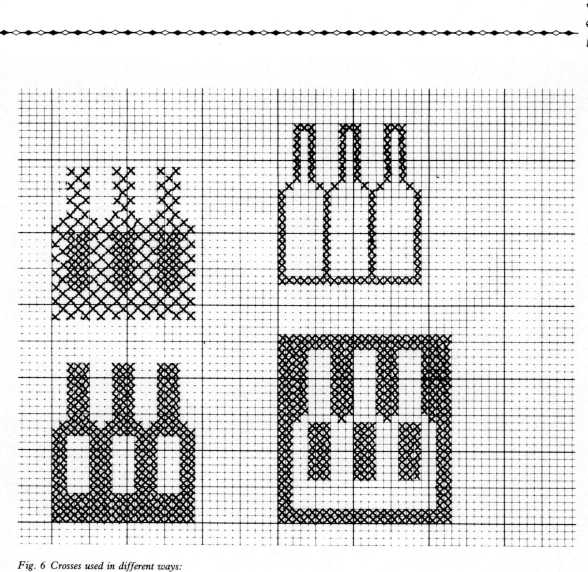

Fig. 6 *Crosses used in different ways:*

a. *Spaced and solid*

b. *As solid forms*

c. *As outlines*

d. *As background*

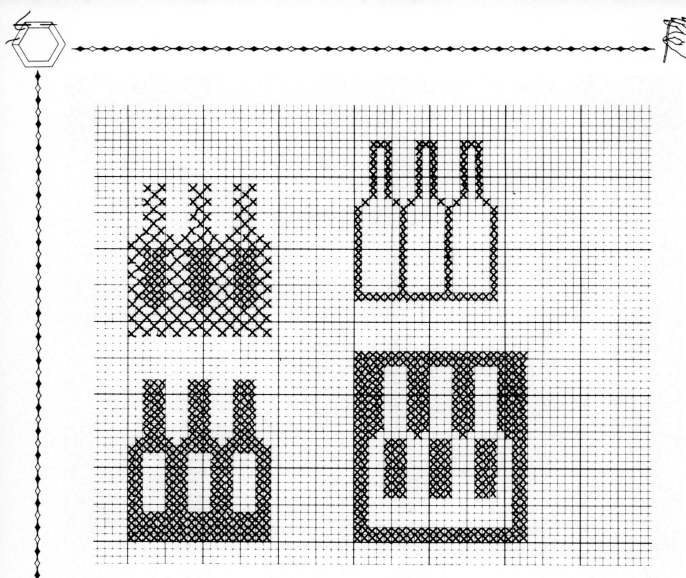

Fig. 6 Crosses used in different ways:

a. Spaced and solid

b. As solid forms

c. As outlines

d. As background

6

FABRIC

Evenweave

Fabrics with the same number of warp and weft threads in a square are called evenweaves. They are generally made of cotton or linen and can be expensive. However, they are colourfast and washable and have a clearly visible weave which facilitates the easy counting of threads. Choose a fabric to suit your own eyesight – 20 to 24 threads to 1in. (2.5cm) is average.

Open weave

Exciting and varied results can be obtained using any fabric which has a weave open enough to be clearly seen – such as hessian, scrim, hopsack and some man-made fabrics. Many dress and furnishing fabrics have a suitable 'linen-type' of weave. Remember, however, that where the warp and weft is of uneven thickness, the cross-stitches will no longer come out square – and this will affect the final shape of the design. A square motif for the centre of a square cushion, for example, would only work on an evenweave fabric.

Close weave

Cross-stitch can also be worked on any closely woven, or even non-woven fabric, where the threads cannot be counted – fabrics such as silk, fine cotton or denim, leather, suede or felt – if you choose one of the following methods:

Evenweave method of transfer

(a) Tack a spare piece of evenweave fabric on to the chosen fabric, being careful to match the grain, and work the design on the counted threads of the evenweave, but going through both fabrics. A sharp needle will be required for this. Make sure that the piece of evenweave fabric is a little larger than the cross-stitch design, as when the stitching is complete the threads of the top fabric are carefully pulled out, one by one, leaving the even cross-stitches on the fabric beneath. It is

important to work with a firm even tension – if it is too tight there can be difficulty pulling out the threads, and if it is too loose the stitches look untidy when the threads have been withdrawn. It is worth working a sample piece with identical fabrics to check the tension before starting work.

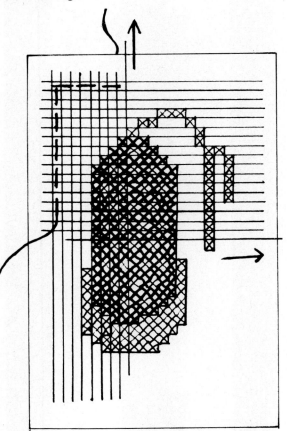

Fig. 7 Design worked over a piece of evenweave, tacked to closely woven fabric, with threads being withdrawn.

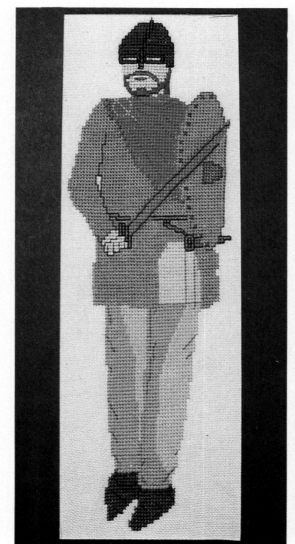

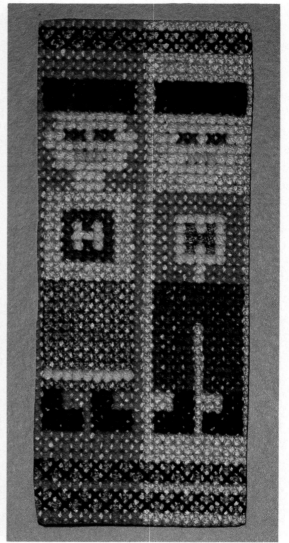

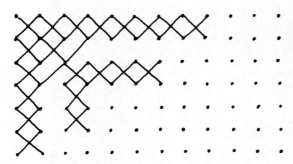

Fig. 8 Crosses worked on a dot pattern.

Dot method of transfer

(b) Measure out the distance required for each cross-stitch with a ruler, and mark the fabric with dots, using one of the 'water soluble' embroidery marking pencils. Work the stitches using the dots as a guide – when the pattern is complete the dots can be removed with a damp cloth.

(c) The same method can be achieved by using one of the commercially available smocking dot transfers – they can be ironed on to the fabric, but the article has to be washed to remove the marks.

(d) Instead of ironing the transfer on to the fabric, sheer fabrics can be laid over the dot pattern and marked with a water soluble pencil.

Page 8:
Viking – *a design drawn out on graph paper, where each square represents a cross-stitch, and then counted out on to bleached linen and worked with Danish Flower threads using cross-stitch and Holbein stitch (Birthe Crawford).*

Page 8:
Peruvian couple – *worked in thick wool on binca fabric, a quickly completed piece taken from a traditional Peruvian design (Audrey Ormrod).*

Page 9:
Canoeist – *worked on fine canvas with a variety of threads in different size cross and half cross-stitch (Sheila de Kretser).*

(e) If the fabric is translucent rather than transparent, tape the dot pattern on to a window with double-sided tape and press the fabric on top – the dots can then be seen against the light and marked on as before.

Checks

Fabrics with small checks such as gingham can be used for cross-stitch by basing the crosses upon the coloured squares rather than counting the threads.

PREPARATION OF FABRICS

Iron the fabric first, allowing for a generous area around the required dimension for making up. If the fabric is evenweave, withdraw a thread vertically and horizontally and cut along these lines to ensure that the grain is straight. Bind or oversew the edges to prevent fraying while working.

THREADS

There is a whole range of threads available for embroidery and your choice will depend on the fabric and the purpose of the article. For durable and washable articles, cotton or linen thread should be used on cotton or linen fabric. Cotton thread is either twisted or stranded. Some workers prefer the twisted cotton as it is firm and round and makes a precise cross-stitch. Stranded cotton, on the other hand, has six easily separated strands, and cross-stitch can be worked with any number – when using more than one strand cut the required length and then separate each strand before laying them together again. This ensures that the strands lie smoothly and produce a better stitch.

Texture

For decorative articles, there is virtually no limit to the choice of thread, and modern fabrics afford scope for experiment with threads of all kinds. These can vary from fine silk, wool, crochet threads, weaving and knitting yarns, raffia, string and strips of fabric – the latter could be worked quickly for a large hanging, or a sturdy bag on coarse fabric or binca. The Peruvian couple (shown on page 8) were quickly worked in thick wool on binca fabric – (binca is a coarse soft canvas-like fabric).

Interesting results can also come from a contrast in texture, and this is often preferable to a change in colour. The texture and weight of thread can be altered, or a shiny thread can be worked next to a matt one.

A very subtle effect can be achieved by stitching with threads pulled from the background fabric.

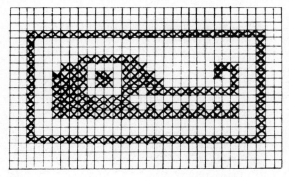

Fig. 9 Crocodile head design.   Samples overleaf.

Samples

It is useful to work samples of ten-stitch squares to see the effect of the thread and fabric together. Samples should be labelled and kept, as they can be a most useful source of reference.

An illustration of the different effects of fabric and thread on the same design is shown in the sampler on page 12. The design consists of a stylized crocodile head – the number of stitches (crosses) is exactly the same in each sample, but the results vary considerably according to the fabric and thread used:

1. Stranded cotton on linen scrim (the kind used for window-cleaning).

2. Fine silk on fine canvas – to give the effect of an illuminated manuscript, the canvas was first sprayed with gold paint.
3. Cotton threads on gingham.
4. Narrow strips of fabric on binca for the crocodile head – the background worked diagonally in a variety of wools.

NEEDLES

When you are working on evenweave fabric, use a blunt tapestry needle which will slip easily between the threads.

A closely woven fabric requires a sharp needle to pierce the threads. Use a crewel needle for this, as it has a long enough eye to take several strands of thread.

For suede or leather, use a leather needle with a triangular point. All these needles come in different sizes, the higher the number the finer the needle. Choose a size which will take the thread and which will pass easily through the fabric.

FRAMES

To maintain a regular and even tension on the stitches, a frame may be found necessary. A ring frame can be

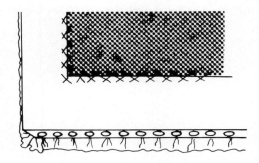

Fig. 10 Home-made frame.

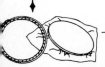

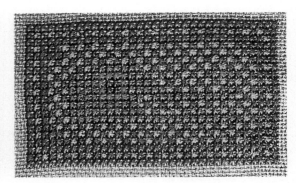

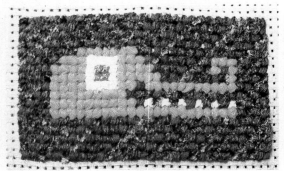

Crocodile head designs – *captions in text (Audrey Ormrod).*

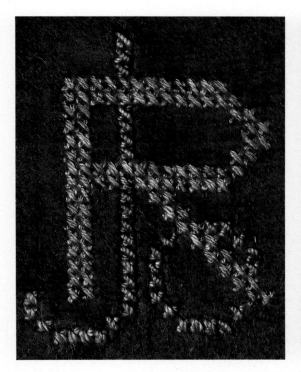

Monogram on suede – 'Jo. R' worked with space-dyed stranded cotton and cotton perle (Pamela Watts).

Monogram on linen – 'T.M.' worked in stranded cotton on evenweave linen (Pamela Watts).

used as long as the design can be wholly contained within it – moving a ring about distorts both the threads and the fabric.

Use a slate frame or an old picture frame for larger pieces of work. When using a frame, the stitch will have to be made in two movements, the needle passing through from front to back and then through to the front again.

DESIGN

Cross-stitch designs are traditionally geometric and can be worked out on graph paper, one square on the paper representing one cross-stitch on the fabric. The crosses on the graph paper can be drawn in different colours so that the final effect can be seen at a glance and altered if necessary.

Remember that the size of the design on the graph paper will not necessarily bear any relation to the size of the stitched design on the fabric. Before completing a large design on graph paper, work a small sample on the proposed fabric to determine the scale.

It is not difficult to evolve your own designs from drawings or pictures in books and magazines. Lay a piece of tracing graph paper over the chosen area and mark in the squares, remembering that curved lines will become stepped and somewhat angular in appearance.

BACKGROUNDS

Simple isolated shapes or motifs can be linked together by adding a background pattern. In traditional Assisi work the background is filled in with rows of crosses in a solid colour, and the actual motifs are outlined with Holbein stitch and left blank. Experiment with patterning the background with soft colour in bands of different widths, or filling in parts of the background with a thin thread – say one strand in a dark colour – to give a shadow effect. A background can be lightly filled with a grid of lines, horizontal or vertical or diagonal, and with two colours a 'woven' over-and-under effect can be achieved.

An interesting background will often throw up the design, or if worked in bold patterns or bright colours will form part of it. Ideas for the use of different backgrounds can be seen on page 16

COLOUR

Traditionally peasant and Assisi cross-stitch were worked in strong bold colours, and more recently naturalistic colours have been favoured for floral motifs. However, now that there are so many threads and fabrics to choose from, and many embroiderers are evolving their own designs, it is interesting to experiment with the different effects produced by the use of colour.

Try using six strands in the needle, each of a different colour – this has a lovely subtle effect.

A bolder treatment is to work with a number of needles (see picture on page 17) each threaded with a different colour, working one cross only at a time in each colour. Keep the needles on the surface as you work to prevent a tangle of threads underneath. A mottled effect can be achieved using just two or three colours in near tones and working a few stitches of each at a time.

BORDERS

Borders can be built up in stages. A simple line of crosses, straight, stepped or V-shaped, will make a

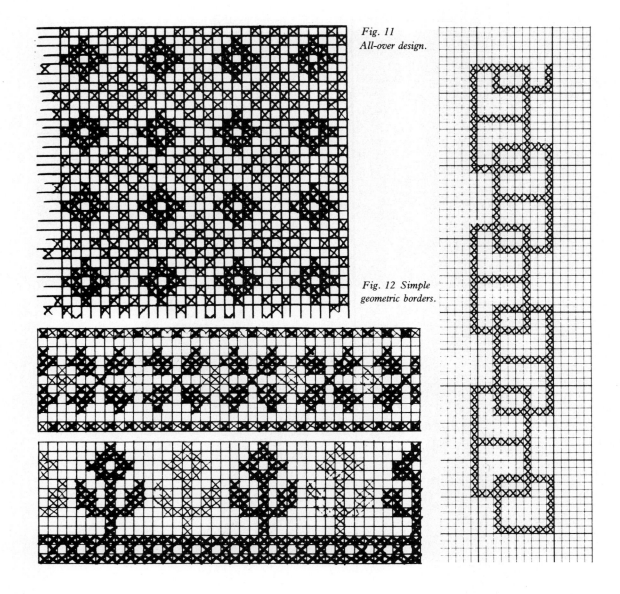

Fig. 11
All-over design.

Fig. 12 Simple
geometric borders.

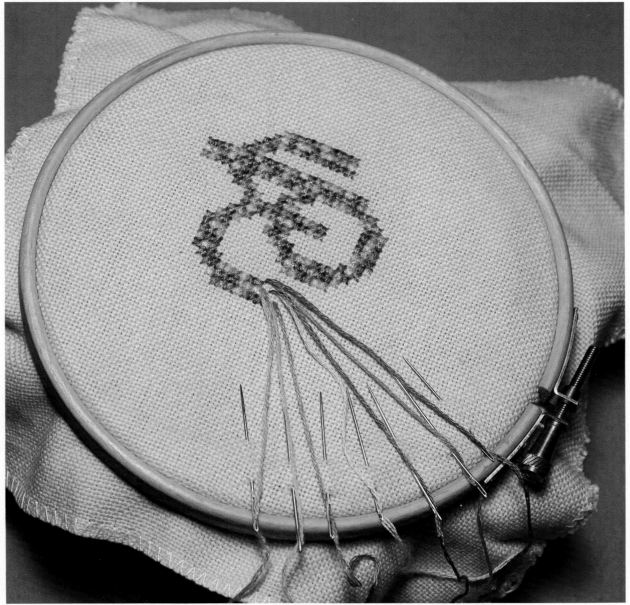

basis on which to build. Alternatively, squares and
rectangles may be arranged to make interesting border
patterns – these can be regular or irregular, and can be
worked either as outlines linked together or as solid
shaped filled with stitches.

Corners

These can be treated in different ways:
1. A different motif can be inserted at the corners – but
it should bear some relation to the rest of the design.
2. The borders are continued to the edge, the stitches
at the intersection being of a different colour combination to the rest.
3. The pattern is bisected diagonally. The best way of
doing this is to hold a small mirror diagonally across the
border pattern. The reflection will show how the design
will continue in the other direction. Move the mirror
along the border slowly, until the most pleasing
arrangement is found.

Page 16:
1. Striped background – *squares and rectangles shown up
against stripes, worked on floba linen with stranded cotton
(Dorle Dawson).*
2. Blended colour background – *circles worked on
Hardanger fabric in stranded cottons, the background with a
varying number of coloured strands in the needle (Doreen
Bibby).*
3. Graduated background – *windmill sails shown against
diminishing strength of colour and tone, worked on evenweave
linen with single strands of cotton and silk (Pamela Nether).*
4. Shadow background – *a cougar outlined against an
Assisi type of shaped background, worked on Hardanger linen
with Perle numbers 5 and 8, and various thicknesses of
stranded cotton (Penny Kramer).*

Page 17:
Sample of multi-coloured cross-stitch – *showing seven
threads in use with separate needles. (Pamela Watts)*

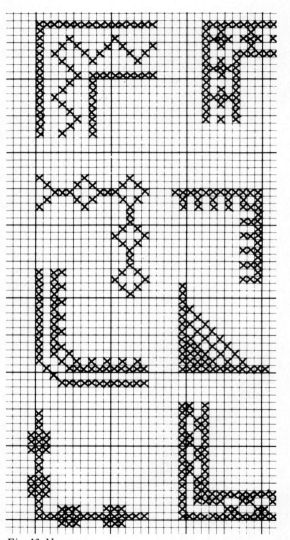

Fig. 13 Narrow corners.

Fig. 14 *Different treatments for deep corners.*

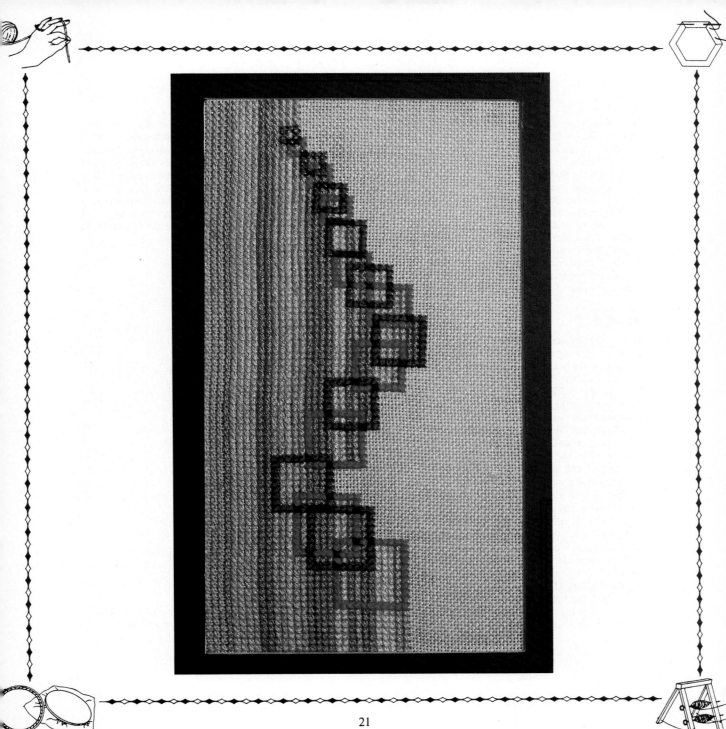

SCALE

The final size of the design on the fabric can be worked out as follows:

1. Work 2cms of crosses of the desired size on the chosen fabric.
2. Count the number of crosses.
3. Count the number of crosses on the length and breadth of the design.
4. Divide No. 3 by No. 2. This will give the measurements in centimetres.

Patterns can be enlarged or reduced by altering the size of the crosses, or by choosing a finer or coarser fabric. Sometimes these methods may result in a drastic alteration in size of the design, in which case it may be better to alter the dimensions of the design.

PLACING

Count the squares of your design, mark the centre point on all four sides, and join these with a horizontal and a vertical line. Count the threads on your fabric, mark the centres on each side, and tack a horizontal and a vertical line. When you begin working in cross-stitch from your design it will then be easy to start from the central point.

Where motifs, corners or borders are planned, mark the outlines with running stitch. This will show you the extent and positioning of the stitchery before you begin, and will allow any alteration to be made before starting work.

Where a design has to be counted out exactly, count across the fabric and mark every tenth thread with a pin. If necessary, tack along these lines both vertically and horizontally to form a grid on the fabric. This can be useful for the positioning of motifs and as a check on the progress of a complicated pattern.

Motifs should be worked from the centre outwards. Border patterns can be worked outwards from the centre point of each side. Corner motifs start in the corner and are worked outwards.

ASSISI WORK

This is a variation of cross-stitch embroidery whereby the design is left unworked and the background is filled with cross-stitch. The design must have a good silhouette, and traditionally it often consisted of fabulous animals worked in outline in double running-stitch with a background entirely covered with cross-stitch in one colour. This is an interesting technique to adapt to contemporary design, illustrated by the sample of architecture on page 20 where one design is worked in cross-stitch and one in Assisi work.

Page 20:
Farm buildings – *two versions of the same design, one worked in cross-stitch and the other in Assisi work. Even-weave linen and stranded cottons. (Clare Emery)*

Page 21:
Linked squares – *design based upon a photograph of open doors, worked on evenweave linen using various thicknesses of stranded cotton (Penny Kramer).*

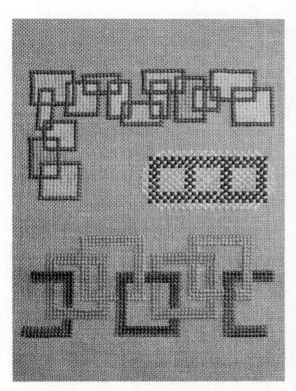

Borders and corners – *Linked squares and rectangles worked in stranded cotton on evenweave linen, which could be used as straight border patterns or easily adapted to turn a corner (Pamela Watts).*

FREE CROSS-STITCH

A recent development in the technique of cross-stitch has been a much freer use of the stitch – varying the size, shape, colour and methods of grouping – which can be very successful and exciting. Crosses can be worked in blocks or rhythmic lines, or as a single stitch scattered freely over the work in a variety of colour, size and thread, which can produce very lively effects.

Blocks of stitches on counted thread fabrics

Varying the solidity of the 'blocks' is often much more effective than changing the colour and it gives the finished work more impact and cohesion.

There are several ways in which different densities can be achieved.

1. Use different thicknesses of thread – this method is somewhat limited by the size of the weave.
2. Vary the size and spacing of the crosses.
3. Use different depths of one colour – that is to say, deeper or lighter tones. Commercial threads often do not give sufficient variety of tone, and it is useful to be able to dye one's own threads. Use a commercial dye and make up according to the instructions. Use a tiny amount and dye a selection of threads in all densities – as the solution weakens the colours will change and fade. Remember that when the threads are rinsed and dried they will be much paler than they appeared in the dyebath.

Single stitches on counted thread fabrics

Single stitches can be worked in one colour but in varying density to give the effect of light and shade.

Crosses may also be worked singly in many different colours – the Impressionist painters used dots of primary and secondary colours to vibrating effect, and this technique can be adapted to cross-stitch, using both colour and texture, and even oversewing some of the crosses many times.

When crosses are worked singly and often far apart care must be taken to count threads to make sure the

stitches eventually link up on the appropriate lines. When a variety of colours are in use, keep those temporarily out of use on the front of the work until needed – this saves a tangle of threads at the back.

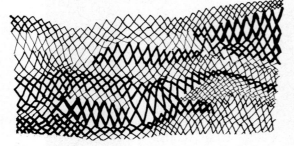

Fig. 15 Rhythmic lines of crosses in a variety of threads.

Page 24:
Field of poppies – *the background fabric is a loosely woven cotton which permitted the use of really thick threads, including strips of nylon fabric for the poppies and raffia for the fence. It was worked freely from the drawing, and many of the crosses overlap (Audrey Ormrod).*

Page 25:
Roofs of Florence – *colour was very important in creating the atmosphere of hot Italian roofs and hard shadows. The terracotta threads were dyed in shavings of Brazil wood. The dark areas in the shadows were the same threads as in the sunshine, but they had been quickly plunged into a grey dye. The 'blocks' were originally planned in cut paper, keeping fairly close to the required colours – they were then re-drawn on graph paper to ensure that the structure of the buildings would fit together. The embroidery was worked using both design sheets (Audrey Ormrod).*

Free stitching on closely woven fabrics

Here there are no limitations of counting threads, and no restrictions on the size and shape of the stitch, so that crosses can be used in rhythmic lines, singly, or grouped at random. With a sharp needle crosses can be made in rhythmic lines that have a flowing quality – these can be used for a whole work, or as a filling stitch in certain areas, perhaps in combination with other stitches. Getting a rhythm into your stitching comes more easily if it is worked in the hand rather than in a frame. Random crosses can be dotted about quite freely like spots of paint – there is no counting threads – the crosses may be in any variety of shape or size and they may even overlap to build up a texture. To a certain extent, the size of the weave will determine the thickness of the threads – but the free approach makes cross-stitch into a flexible and exciting technique.

DESIGN FOR FREE CROSS-STITCH

From the beginning, consider whether the embroidery is to be in monotone, or in a limited number of colours, or in a great variety of colour. Colour and tone are both vital as cross-stitch is crisp and formal and shows every degree of colour and tonal gradation.

If the design is to be adapted from a coloured original, it is sometimes helpful to take a photocopy to reveal the 'weight' of each colour – tonal values can be seen more clearly in black and white and through half-closed eyes, and they can be achieved by using one colour of thread in many variations of thickness and size of stitch or in a variety of colours considering the 'weight' of each. Ideas often spring from detailed scenes, or from drawings or photos that are far too complicated to embroider – and although they remain the source of inspiration, such designs need to be simplified and adapted, and in this way they also become the embroiderer's own personal interpretation.

Simplifying designs

A way of planning the broad outline of the design is to make a collage of it in paper – either in black and white newsprint, or in colour pages from magazines. Cut or tear the shapes of the design – they may follow the idea of the original but will be greatly simplified – and lay the pieces on a background. Try both cutting and tearing, the subject itself will sometimes dictate which is better. Half-close your eyes and consider the tonal effects. Move the shapes around. Leave the design for a while for consideration. Try a paper frame around it, it may look better with different proportions.

TRANSLATING DESIGNS INTO CROSS-STITCH

Using graph paper

If the design has geometric shapes – such as buildings, lettering or vehicles – it is better to work it out first on graph paper and then transfer the design to the fabric by counting the threads. One square of graph paper represents one cross.

Flowing shapes can be drawn or traced directly on to graph paper, and then filled in with crosses.

More complicated shapes can be transferred by the method described on page 14, where graph tracing paper is laid over the design and marked in crosses – this is a good way to work out tonal values as the darkest areas can be filled up first with heavy dark crosses, working up to the palest areas which can be very faintly marked.

Painting on the fabric

For designs which consist of rounded shapes that do not need to be symmetrical, such as trees or figures, you can save the counting by painting the design straight on to the material. From the beginning it must be decided whether to paint in strong colours that will show through the stitches and be part of the finished effect, or to dilute the paint so that you only get the faintest impression on the fabric as a guide for stitching. There are two methods by which a design can be painted on to the fabric:

1. By painting the design directly on to the fabric with fabric paint or crayons – this assumes a certain amount of aptitude, and it is difficult to control the exact tones.

2. By using transfer dyes to make a coloured 'transfer' which is then ironed on to the fabric. For this method the design may be drawn on to tracing paper, the paper is then turned over and the colours (dyes) are then painted on the reverse. When the painting is dry, the paper is placed paint side down on the fabric and the design is ironed off on to the fabric. This method enables you to get the design exactly as you want it before transferring it, and by painting on the back the design will come out the right way round.

Page 28:
John at sixteen – *a portrait of the author's son based on photographs and sketches. The inspiration for the work came from the paintings of the Impressionists, especially Seurat. The technique of using dots of primary and secondary colours laid side by side is translated into cross-stitch in single stranded cotton on an evenweave linen. (Audrey Ormrod)*

Page 29:
Kelly's bar – *the aim was to suggest the contrasting atmosphere of the bright solid outside of the building, and the view through the doorway into the dark, smoky and crowded bar. A further description of this work is on page 30 (Audrey Ormrod)*

'Kelly's bar'

This embroidery embodies the methods described above. The design was originally evolved from a collage of cut and torn paper; the geometric parts – such as the building, the lettering and the doorway – were planned on squared paper and worked in large cross-stitches in wool, soft cotton and raffené on binca. The interior of the bar was painted on fine canvas which was tacked in place, and the edges hidden in the stitches of the surround – the canvas was worked with cross-stitch in a fine thread.

FINISHING

This process of embroidery is very important as it can make or mar the finished work. Ironing should be avoided as far as possible, especially on the stitched areas. However, table linen and clothing will need to be ironed and this should be done on a well-padded board. Press lightly with a steam iron on the wrong side and the stitches will not be flattened. Cross-stitch embroidery rarely distorts the fabric, but decorative work can be returned to its original crispness by being stretched.

STRETCHING

Small pieces of work may be pinned out on an ironing board as taut as possible, with the edges at right angles. Lay a damp cloth on top and leave until dry.

Larger pieces of work must be pinned with rustless drawing pins or tacks on to a board with some layers of sheeting or blotting-paper underneath (make sure this extends beyond the embroidery). Cover with a damp cloth and leave until dry.

MOUNTING

There are many ways of finishing work but it usually involves mounting the fabric over stiff card or hardboard. A pleasant soft effect can be achieved by first glueing a layer of thin foam rubber, wadding or a piece of blanket on to the board. Lay the embroidery over this, stretch the surplus fabric over the back of the board – holding it in place with pins stuck round the edge while you check the positioning – and then secure the fabric on the back by lacing it tightly to and fro with strong thread in both directions.

Alternatively the fabric at the back can be glued or stapled in position.

Padding is not suitable for framing where glass in used.

FRAMING

Consider carefully whether a frame is necessary, and, if so, what width and colour of frame will best enhance the embroidery. Spend time setting the work against various papers, fabrics and frames to ensure the best possible result.

Page 31:
Opposite: working diagram of 'Kelly's Bar'.

☒ bright red ⊡ gold

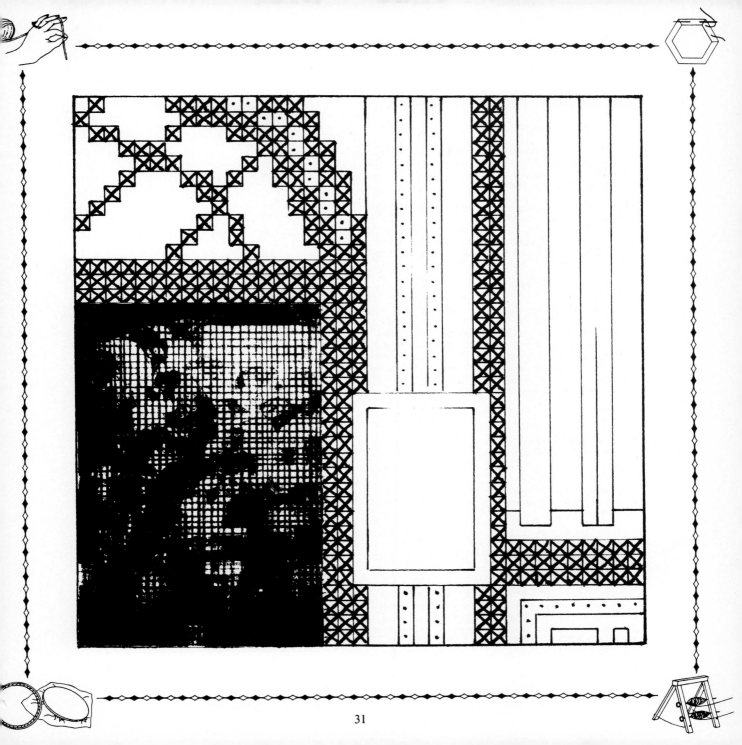

Acknowledgements

Series editor: Kit Pyman

Text and original art material on Cross-stitch techniques by
Pamela Watts, and on Free Cross-stitch by Audrey Ormrod
Drawings and diagrams by Jan Messent
Photographs by Search Press Studios

Text, illustrations, arrangement and typography copyright
© Search Press Limited 1984

First published in Great Britain in 1984 by Search Press
Limited, Wellwood, North Farm Road, Tunbridge Wells,
Kent TN2 3DR.

Reprinted 1986, 1988, 1989

ISBN 0 85532 453 8

Made and printed in Spain by A. G. Elkar, S. Coop.
Autonomía, 71 - 48012-Bilbao - Spain

Front cover:
Striped background – *squares and rectangles shown up
against stripes, worked on flobas linen with stranded cotton.
(Dorle Dawson)*

Inside front cover:
Design of four rams' heads – *in traditional Assisi work
technique, using two strands of stranded cotton on a fine
evenweave fabric. (Clare Emery)*

Back cover:
Poppies – *inspired by a lovely bunch of scarlet poppies, the
design was worked out freely, drawing with coloured pencils
on graph paper. A small piece of blue evenweave linen
provided the background, and it was worked in stranded cotton
and coton à broder (Audrey Ormrod).*